FEDERAL BRITAIN
Replacing The Westminster Establishment with a Federal Constitution.

By Professor Stephen Haseler.
Edited and formatted by Junade Ali.
Published by the Reform Foundation.

Editor's Note

With the UK still shaking from the recent Scottish independence referendum and with promises from political party leaders still to be delivered; undoubtably we are on the precipice of constitutional reform in Britain. Though with more constitutional questions to answer after the referendum than before it, the direction of change is still to be determined.

Professor Haseler argues we must bring about enormous reform on these islands by introducing a new federal constitution fit for the UK, reviewing every institution with no stone left unturned. Writing about Scottish independence as still a possibility he proposes that 'if we avoid fundamental constitutional change the union will break-up within the next few years'.

The former 'Deputy Mayor' of London, a founder member of the SDP (now merged into the Liberal Democrats), a former Labour General Election candidate and a regular contributor on TV and radio; Professor Stephen Haseler has a political history to be envious of.

Having held visiting professorships at several American universities including Georgetown University and Johns Hopkins University; he is currently the Emeritus Professor of Government and Director of the Global Policy Institute in the City of London (at LMU). He is the author of many books on British and European politics including The English Tribe, Meltdown UK and The Grand Delusion.

Politics should be the way in which people collectively take decisions on the type of society they want to live in. But too many people feel detached from politics – they do not see it as being relevant to them and they do not believe they have the power to influence events. Politics has become tainted by scandals and democracy has been undermined by activities of commercial and other powerful interest groups. It is imperative that confidence in politics as the way of taking national and local decisions is rebuilt.

— Dr Ken Ritchie (Reform Foundation Chair)

It is my personal belief that if we are to accept that democracy is the best form of collective decision making that we as humanity have arrived at, it must follow that our goal should be to enhance it and reduce the perversive effects of those who seek to undermine it. The brutality of the system is hidden in its complexity. When more than half of citizens in this country voted against their winning MP, when a government with the constitutional power to go to war can be elected with just over one third of the popular vote and when we have more unelected Peers in the House of Lords than MPs in the House of Commons; it is clear this system is not fit for purpose.

The Reform Foundation seeks to build a better democracy; passing power to the people by promoting popular debate about democracy. Join us: reformfoundation.org.

This book features an introduction and 2 essays from Professor Stephen Haseler's upcoming book "Our Broken Kingdom" and a paper on a practical need from a written constitution by Graham Allen MP published earlier in 2014 by the Reform Foundation.

— Junade Ali (Editor)

Federal Britain   **Page 2**

    Editor's Note   4

    Introduction   5

    The Failure of a Political Class   10

    The Road To A Written Federal Constitution   47

War Making and the Rights of Parliament   **Page 56**

ISBN: 978-1-326-11271-4
© 2015 Reform Foundation Limited. All Rights Reserved.

Introduction

In this book I argue that the United Kingdom and its Westminster system of government has a major design flaw; buffeted by high winds from Scotland and from the European Union, it is no longer fit for the purpose of governing the British Islands. With an 'anéien regime' of unelected, obscure and obscurantist, institutions, governments cobbled together with minority votes from the electorate, and an elite, or political class, increasingly unrepresentative and remote (and, indeed, seen by growing numbers of their fellow citizens as corrupt, catering only to the wealthy and privileged); it has a serious democratic deficit.

I also suggest that the central problem with our Westminster political class, or the 'establishment' as it is now often called, is its inability to adjust. Addicted to the old fashioned notion of its own 'sovereignty' it now finds itself unable and unwilling to adjust to the real world all around it; whether these be the pressures of 'globalisation', the EU or social change in Britain itself. Unsurprisingly the whole country now faces a real constitutional and political crisis, not just of this class, but of the Westminster state itself. Decades of complacency and arrogance have now led us to the point where the nation and its union may well be dissolved within the next few years, entailing ramifications for the stability of the country and its people.

This arrogance and complacency was on display for all to see during the Scottish independence referendum campaign of 2014. The Westminster establishment after having treated the Scots with disdain, when it seemed that the 'Yes' vote might carry the day, they panicked. Westminster's three political leaders - David Cameron, Nick Clegg and Ed Miliband - at the very last moment, dropped all other business, rushed north of the border and offered the Scots by way of a 'solemn vow' what amounted to a form of 'Home Rule', should they vote 'No' that is. Then, immediately following the referendum (and the victory for the 'No' vote) British Prime Minister Cameron appeared outside Downing to make another ad hoc constitutional announcement, this time that that his party would be seeking to abandon the union principle of the equality of all MPs by establishing 'English Votes For English Laws'. What this meant is that, should Scottish, Welsh and Northern Irish MPs be denied full voting status in the Westminster Parliament then the budget of a British government (say a Labour government with a majority of British MPs backing it) could be voted down by a majority of English MPs.

What was incredible and revealing about this episode, was that these three Westminster leaders felt they had the lone right to make such momentous decisions, a last minute offer 'on the back of an envelope' and a sudden proposal for *'English Votes for English Laws'*. In other words they felt free to to use the 'constitution' as little more than a political plaything or a negotiating tool. Of course, the sad truth is that the three Westminster leaders did *in fact* have every right to use the 'constitution' in such a cavalier manner; our much revered unwritten Westminster system (the 'Mother of Parliaments' no less) was designed specifically to allow its elite, without reference to the people in any way, to change the basic rules at will.

Thus, in 2014 the stability of the country was threatened not just by separatist forces north of the border, or nationalists south of the border, but by the centralised Westminster political class itself. My thesis here is that unless we fundamentally restructure our system of government and open up our political class we are surely heading for a break-up of the union.

Indeed, let us posit the following scenario, one that is not at all fanciful. Scots voters feel deceived (either by unsatisfactory extra powers or by their MPs at Westminster being downgraded). The poll ratings of the SNP rise considerably as does SNP membership. The Leader of the SNP declares that should her party win the Westminster general election or the Assembly election in 2016 then they will demand a another referendum (with an implicit threat that if Westminster should refuse them then they will arrange a unilateral yes/no referendum regardless of what the Westminster government says about it). The 300 year union would then be over: Scotland becomes independent in 2018, motions are passed in the Welsh Assembly to go the same way as Scotland, the issue of Northern Ireland's future position is raised. Following this agitation begins in Northern Ireland to keep the province linked to England and counter-agitation begins in support of linking the province to the republic in the south, this could cause Catholic-Protestant tensions to rise throughout Ireland and in Glasgow and Liverpool. As the stability and social fabric of the British union are now threatened, foreign investors begin to pull their money out of sterling.

Of course none of this may happen. The attraction of Scottish independence may well wane and following an economic upturn the threat to both the union and the stability of the country could fade away. Yet, herewith another scenario: Eurosceptic forces succeed in securing a referendum on British membership of the EU in 2017 with the result showing that a majority of English voters have voted to leave, whereas a majority of Scottish and Welsh voters have voted to stay. As Downing Street prepares the country to leave the EU, the Scottish Parliament and the Welsh Assembly vote to stay in the EU; and the Scots and Welsh, through their parliaments, start fateful proceedings to become independent and negotiate with the EU about staying. England, Scotland and Wales go their separate ways.

Of course, again, none of this may happen. Yet the fact that these scenarios are now at least plausible shows how very fragile the political and social stability of these islands have become.

In this book I look at how we got into this sorry and dangerous state. Of course, much always depends on economics; there can be little doubt that the global financial crisis and its aftermath of austerity has contributed mightily to an all-pervasive western sense of failure and accounts for much of the disenchantment with our 'establishment' and its Westminster system. However, Britain's establishment cannot avoid the blame for the global financial market system which crashed so spectacularly in 2007-8. This was in large part the product of the Thatcher-Reagan neoliberal deregulation revolution of the 1980s in which Britain's neoconservative elite took such a leadership role.

Of course, it might well be argued that I am far too unkind to our political class. After all, it is certainly the case that there is a wider crisis of leadership and legitimacy throughout the west; but I still hold to the view that in Britain, certainly compared to other advanced countries, has a special problem as our elites are drawn from such a socially and educationally narrow and conformist class. It is worth asking: in what other country would so many top politicians (and other leaders) have gone not just to one university but to one school?! It surely says something about a country when (as is the case as of writing) the leader of the country, the leader of the largest city and the leader of the official, established church are all old Etonians. It also says something when so many in Britain's leadership positions (from politics to media to financial services) were privately-schooled then going to the 2 same universities in a nation overwhelmingly state educated. These institutions are redolent with past greatness, with an elite with such a narrow background. One redolent with the culture of past national and imperial greatness, it is hardly surprising that our 'constitution' and institutions form a kind of 'ancient régime' reminiscent with imperial trappings uniquely unable to adjust to the modern world: including the centralised Westminster state itself, the Monarchy, the Lords, the Commonwealth, the established Anglican church.

This analysis of how we got to where we are helps in sketching out where we go from here and what now could follow. Much of this centres around the great constitutional issues raised by the 'English Question'. For instance: as the UK fractures where does England fit in? What about an English Parliament? And English City-Regions? What about 'the North' which, in an English Parliament, might be dominated by the City of London and the dormitory suburbs in Surrey? And what of London? These are great issues in themselves, but much depends on the question of an English identity.

Also, in this book, I try and outline how these great constitutional issues now facing the country can only be properly resolved by establishing a written federal constitution for the British Islands, of course this kind of radical constitutional change is easier said than done. Yet in the essay on *'The Road to a Written Federal Constitution'* I hope to show how in fact we can move from the now widely-accepted case for a federal constitution to actually implementing one.

I would like to thank the committee of The Reform Foundation for their help in the production of this book and Junade for his design prowess. The views are mine and mine alone.

Stephen Haseler
London 2014

The Failure of a Political Class

Success

The United Kingdom was founded in 1707 by the Act of Union between England and Scotland which built upon the earlier 1603 union of the crowns of the two nations. Over the next three centuries this new nation-state became one of the world's most impressive success stories as it rose from the ranks of the middling European powers to lead a great world empire.

As the state succeeded so its 'constitution' and institutions flourished too. Westminster's unitary state formed of its interlinked nexus of monarchy, Lords, established church, Privy Council and House of Commons at the height of empire in late Victorian times not only became entrenched but assumed an almost sacred standing. Reverence for this has lasted well into the present day. Not only exalted; Westminster's 'Mother of Parliaments' was copied around the world as with the Westminster state, so too with its political class and wider 'establishment'. Confident rulers for confident times.

The Westminster System: Design Flaw

That was then. Some hundred years on from the height of empire our constitution and our rulers, today's Westminster system, have been slow to adjust both to geo-political changes abroad and to social changes at home. In Dean Acheson's famous phrase Britain 'has lost an empire, not yet found a role', and today is no longer even a 'great power' in the old sense. Yet this middling European country has a constitution and associated institutions still redolent with imperial grandeur. 'Mother of Parliaments', monarchy, peers and an established church with its world-wide Anglican community simply do not fit the times.

At home, today's Westminster, with its highly centralised unitary constitution, seems unconnected with the modern reality of national, regional, class and ethnic differences in Britain. As do its elites (still pompously and ludicrously calling themselves 'honourable' and 'noble') who seem to become increasingly divorced from everyday lives once inside the system. The old and easy arrogance and complacency of imperial times still run through many veins, qualities that nearly lost Scotland in September 2014.

In one sense modern Britain should be well-equipped to adjust to change. Our evolutionary system and our vaunted pragmatic elite should be able to react and adjust to change relatively quickly. But that is on paper. In truth, however, we still see the world through the prism of our recent past, our time in the sun and our empire. To understand the present backwardness of our constitution and institutions we need to start where the Westminster system started, in the early eighteenth-century.

Modern Westminster's Founders: 'Toffs' Born To Rule

Founded in 1707 the new nation-state, the United Kingdom, had an ignominious beginning- born out of elite corruption and double-dealing. The Presbyterian Church was squared by giving it a special, protected, position in any future union; and the independent Scottish Parliament was effectively sidelined by a motion, moved at the last minute by the 'anti-union' nobleman the Duke of Hamilton, giving power over union negotiations to commissioners appointed by ' the Queen herself. This nobleman, in a nice foretaste of the now well-established Westminster patronage system, subsequently received an English Dukedom, membership of the Order of the Thistle and the Garter, and the post of British Ambassador to

Paris. Daniel Defoe reflected at the time that 'a firmer union of policy with less union of affection has hardly been known in the whole world'. And according to Norman Davies, 'The English were largely indifferent. The Scots were overwhelmingly hostile'.[1]

Born out of shady dealing, the Westminster-led union was, from the very start, a deeply unequal enterprise in which aristocrats ruled. Most of the people living in the new nation-state had nothing to say about its government which was formed, and informed, by the dominant landed interests of the time. This new nation-state was, for all intents and purposes, a polity by, for and of the English aristocracy. During the eighteenth and nineteenth centuries this aristocracy and the aristocratic view of governance (and its associated ideology) not only dominated the state but also permeated down into the broader political culture of the British isles.

Built For Empire: At Home and Abroad

This new nation-state (the United Kingdom of Great Britain, the Westminster-state), this aristocrat-controlled territory and polity, was to see its writ run way beyond the British Isles to reach across the Atlantic and into North America. Settlements, primarily English, in the Americas and the trading posts in East India came over time to be formalised as colonies of this 1707 union. Although Westminster lost its American colonies in the late eighteenth-century, it was to have a second imperial wind in the nineteenth. It started by blowing across the Irish Sea. Ireland was annexed by the UK in 1801 an act recognised by the Act of Union between the UK and Ireland. Although the Irish had representation in the UK Parliament they were, for all intents and purposes, part of the 'internal' or 'domestic' empire run by aristocratic Englishmen.

---

[1] Norman Davies, The Isles: A History, London, 1999, p. 582-583

This 'United Kingdom of Great Britain and Ireland' was the state which saw the high-point of empire. In the process of this imperial expansion the English aristocracy, through the evolving English Parliament, extended its rule beyond the English, Scottish, Welsh and Irish natives in the British isles (few of whom had the vote) and into the colonial possessions. The Cambridge historian John Seeley could argue that 'the drift of [sic] English history' involved both an external empire 'beyond the sea' and an 'internal empire' at home (which he called the 'internal union of the three kingdoms'). Whilst rejecting 'English superiority' he nonetheless saw Britain at home and the empire abroad as one whole polity, a 'mere extension of the English race into other lands...[sic] without conquest.'[2]

This widely held view of the British at home and the colonial masses abroad united as 'subjects' under one 'Crown' (Her Majesty's subjects in Africa and the sub-continent being in some sense on a footing with Her Majesty's subjects in Britain and Ireland) had some validity. Parliament set the laws for both the domestic peoples and the colonial peoples abroad; the British government was the executive authority over both (the Colonial Office dealing with the 'colonials'); the Privy Council and the House of Lords were the arbiters of law for both peoples; and, of course, Queen Victoria and her heirs ruled as head of state ('Empress' as far as the Indians were concerned).

When viewed in this way the British empire was not in essence simply a story of one 'nation' (Britain) or one 'people' (the British) dominating the masses in India and parts of Africa, Asia and the Caribbean. For the disenfranchised 'British people' at home had very little to do with the construction of

---

[2] J.R. Seeley. The Expansion of England, London, 1914, p.78

the imperial system except in the sense that they were recruited to fight and die in the wars of conquest and occupation. Rather the imperial story was one of how a ruling group of English aristocrats and their camp followers established rulership over one third of humanity. Only after the full franchise, some twenty odd years into the twentieth-century did the domestic peoples of this empire begin to use the vote to increase their power and place themselves in a position superior to the colonial subjects.

Of course, some form of elite rulership was the only way to run an empire as large and diverse as the British. This empire simply could not function without a ruling class which was tightly-knit, highly-disciplined, supremely confident, possessed of a sense of superiority linked to a special mission and, of course, ruthless. The English aristocracy was perfect for the task. England's leaders had from feudal times developed habits of rulership, what Kathryn Tidrick called a 'cult of leadership' [3] As it happens this culture of paternalism perfected in feudal times. Lord and peasant culture was appropriate for ruling the growing number of black and brown masses that England's leadership groups controlled. The imperial ethos was redolent with 'aristocratic wisdom' about proper governance; 'firm but fair' paternalism.

Indeed this paternalistic habit of mind became the template not just for governing the colonial masses but the domestic British masses as well. Not surprisingly so. The historian Norman Davies uses the term 'The British Imperial Isles' to describe the process in which domestic Britain and its global empire had become entwined, almost as one. He quotes The Times of India at the coronation of King George V to give a flavour of this idea of oneness: 'Today the eyes of the whole world will be

---

[3] Katherine Tidrick, Empire and The English Character (London 1992)

turned towards the ancient shrine of Westminster where His Most Excellent Majesty George the Fifth will be crowned King of the United Kingdom of Great Britain and Ireland, and of the British Dominions Beyond The Seas, and Emperor of India...The Coronation then, symbolises the growth of the British Nation and the British Empire through twelve centuries.'[4]

Ruling Without Consent

The nineteenth century, the century of empire, saw the emergence of a systematic attempt to provide this empire with a class of rulers. An educational system developed that was geared specifically for rulership over the colonial peoples (and, for good measure, over the British peoples as well).

The military historian Correlli Barnett has identified the nineteenth-century public schools as the breeding ground of this elite. '...most of the administrators of the British Empire, at home and overseas in the 1920 and 1930s, as well as many British business leaders and MPs, were products of the period of its [public schools] ripest development between 1870 and 1900.' And he makes a quite startling claim: that 'except for young Nazis or Communists no class of leaders in modern times has been so subjected to prolonged moulding of character, personality and outlook as British public-school boys in this era'.[5]

The values and lifestyle inculcated in these schools both reflected existing aristocratic life and developed it further. It was a way of thinking and living so powerful that it began to define what it meant to be 'English', producing that most

---

[4] Davies, p. 733

[5] Correlli Barnett, The Collapse of British Power, London, 1972, p. 24

successful global brand 'The English Gentleman'. Though scornful of ideas this culture developed what amounted to an ideology, what the Scottish writer Tom Nairn called the 'Ukanian' ideology of Englishness.

Of course, the manners, values and lifestyle of this Victorian aristocratic class were reflected in the political values of the time- and, crucially, in the 'constitution' and institutions of the empire and the country. The dominant party in Parliament - the Whigs and their Liberal heirs - prided themselves on 'progressive' virtues like good governance, moderation, tolerance, and fairness. Indeed, the Whig ascendancy, these founders of the modern Westminster state, turned Britain into one of the most stable and liberal of nineteenth-century nations. Yet democrats they were not! These aristocrats saw nothing wrong with ruling, from London, indeed from Westminster and Whitehall they ruled millions and millions of people around the globe - white, black, brown, African, Indian, British - without their consent. The mass of peoples, whether domestic or 'colonial', were simply not fit to rule.

Colonial peoples needed a guiding hand. Best to keep governance in the hands of the existing (in this time essentially landed) authority. Indeed, looking back it is striking how all sections of British elite political opinion; Tory, Whig, Liberal, even Radical and later Fabian all ultimately supported the idea of empire and imperial rule.

At home during the late Empire changes in the elite meant that business people and a new middle class were seeking a place at the table too. There began a whole century of appeasement and concessions to social change. In a series of such concessions the franchise was extended, ultimately to all adult men and then in the 1920s to adult women. The key word here is 'concession'; new groups were appeased and the aristocratic liberals in the 'sovereign' Parliament made 'concessions'. Parliament and the Commons are pre-democratic with a pre-democratic culture. They were not forged by democracy or democratic revolutions. They have adapted to democracy; they were not formed by it. Legally and constitutionally the 'sovereign' 'Mother of Parliaments' conceded democracy, but can also take it away, as it did so blatantly when it extended the Parliament Act in 1940 and abolished the GLC in the 1980s.

A Constitution Without Rules

Therein lies the modern problem (and the modern danger). Our present 'constitution' and associated institutions are built for a guided democracy. We, unlike every other modern country, have no basis of a constitution to which we can turn in extremis. When politics go wrong there is no backstop except our good sense, or rather the good sense of the old boys and girls in Westminster (that can sometimes let them down).

Of course there is a British 'constitution', of sorts, handed down to us. But should a citizen or a visitor want to see it, or read it, it is simply not available. Such an enquiry will be met by the following explanation: that the constitution of Britain is made up of many things, past Acts and precedent primarily. In other words our constitution is what Westminster has done in the past and might do in the future. And to the insistent questions which modern man and woman might still impertinently ask: "Is it constitutional?" or "What does the constitution say?" Well, no way of telling! You should consult, not a document (and make up your own mind), but a sage! Such sages, normally academics like Sir Ivor Jennings or more recently Lord Blake, can only 'divine' our constitutional rules because they cannot point to a clear written rules set out in a founding document.

In the Victorian period the idea grew, particularly amongst the Whigs, that writing rules down so that we could all know them, debate them and act within them was far too democratic and egalitarian (indeed rather vulgar). Indeed, in the eyes of the Victorian Parliamentary elite, writing a constitution was an idea born of rebellion in north America and of revolution in France. Westminster's elite was naturally suspicious of written down universal rights like the Universal Declaration of Human Rights. They were considered dangerous. Instead of written constitutional rules which we should all obey (like the Americans or the French had to do) we should instead leave these tiresome 'rules of the road' to be decided by the wisdom of our rulers. Our rulers should be free to react to events and even to change the constitution if they wish.

Such 'freedom' was on display some hundred years later during the Scottish independence crisis of 2014 when Westminster's three main political leaders, panicking over a potential break-up of the union, offered to completely re-write Britain's constitution and grant 'Home Rule to Scotland'. Then, on the day following the vote, the British Prime Minister decided unilaterally to propose what amounted to an 'English Parliament' which could override a future British Prime Minister's budget. Many commentators in early twenty-first century Britain were shocked by such momentous decisions being taken 'on the back of an envelope' and without consultation. Yet the truth is that the three Westminster leaders were acting fully in accordance with 'constitutional principles' handed to us from Victorian (and earlier) times. Like their forebears they did in fact have every right to use the 'constitution' in such a cavalier manner; for our much revered unwritten Westminster system the 'Mother of Parliaments' no less) was designed specifically to allow its elite (without reference to the people in any way) to change the basic rules at will.

Of course in Victorian Britain, and later, it was argued by apologists that allowing our rulers to determine their own rules of government was 'nothing to worry about' because our rulers were liberal and reasonable. On the whole, they were certainly by comparison with some of their opposite numbers in the tumultuous continent on our doorstep. This paternalist Victorian patrimony was fine for the 'Upstairs-Downstairs' society that lasted in Britain right through to the Second World War (and which still evokes nostalgia in the Downton Abbey world propagated by the entertainment industry). The problem for today, though, is that 'Downstairs' has changed, and democratic ideas have broken through. In sum, old-style deference to authority has broken down, and so has trust. Quite simply, we no longer trust our rulers 'to do the right thing' - and rightly so. Without trust we need rules of the road: clearly set out for all to see.

The Three Chambers of the Aristocratic Heart: Monarchy, 'The Mother of Parliaments' and the Established Church.

Deconstructing Westminster's modern unwritten constitution, our 'constitution without consent', will reveal one central truth about the DNA of the primary institutions that rule over us: their very DNA is pre-democratic. Born in feudal times, re-animated and reformed by half-failed rebellions and by the aristocrats who ruled the Victorian empire, the great democratic revolutions that made modern countries out of our competitors have seemingly passed these institutions by. So today, in essence, our great institutions represent a brake upon democracy not an embracing of it. Let us look at the heart of our present institutional set up- the three chambers of the aristocratic, and nostalgic, heart: Westminster's 'Holy Trinity' of Monarchy, the 'Mother of Parliaments' (Lords and Commons) and Established State Church.

Of course these institutions, dripping in the mumbo jumbo of feudal and imperial imagery (gold coaches, their Lordships clad in ermine, the Archbishop and others wearing funny hats) are part of the 'fantasy island' tourist and entertainment industry in the global city of London; it can be argued, and is, that they represent a service to a country which has lost its manufacturing industries and needs tourist income. But at the same time it is not harmless. For these three chambers at the heart of our aristocratic past represent and advance a real non-democratic, even anti-democratic ethos which permeates down-infantalising the people, keeping them in their place. How else can we explain how a major tabloid newspaper can declare a royal baby as 'person of the year'?

At the pinnacle is the monarchy. It should not be forgotten, amidst all the media public relations, that the monarch is not just a celebrity or a tourist attraction. Rather, Elizabeth Windsor is the UK's head of state, and plays a pivotal role in the unwritten constitution, has unrivalled informal political and social power and represents the country, and its subjects, to the world. Yet, this office is 'sacerdotal', it is legitimated not by consent of the people but rather by God. This was a 'constitutional fact' revealed to us all in 2014 after the King of Spain had abdicated largely because of a fall in his popularity and Buckingham Palace let it be known that no abdication here could be expected because Queen Elizabeth inhabits a 'sacerdotal' monarchy, with 'sacred oaths' taken to the almighty, not subject to the whims of public opinion. This extraordinary notion (extraordinary, that is, by modern democratic standards) had also revealed itself in the 1953 coronation ceremony as it is the Archbishop of Canterbury in the name of the deity who lays the crown on the royal head and sprinkles the holy oils. In sum, in an extraordinary affront to the democratic age, the UK monarch owes no allegiance to her people. She inherits the job and holds it as long as she wishes, and is sanctified by the Almighty.

Of course, the British monarchy is not alone. For that other chamber at the heart of our establishment, the Upper House, the House of Lords, stands proudly alongside as a blatant institutional rejection of the democratic age. Populated by a mixture of hereditary peers and life peers, some men and women of achievement, some not, but all are essentially place-men who have been favoured by party leaders. This Upper House, like the monarch, has a serious (though seriously under-reported) role in the Westminster state's executive and law-making system. The Queen, of course, has a formal veto power over all legislation. The House of Lords can, depending on the electoral cycle, effectively hold up legislation, and frustrate the will of the Commons, and 'their Lordships' now play a role, informally through their parties and to some extent through the media, in setting public opinion. One of the delights of our national debate are the number of unelected peers who regularly lecture us (both British and foreigners) on the lack of democratic standards of the EU or developing nations.

Of course, of all the Westminster institutions; the House of Commons remains the one that is congruent with the democratic age, in the sense that it is elected. Well, sort of. One problem is its electoral system in which over three elections 42% of the vote could allow Margaret Thatcher to create an economic and social revolution. And about 33% of the vote can elect a government to run for a full five year term.

The raw truth is that the Commons, our one democratic institution, has been sidelined. It has been sidelined by the powerful combination of the modern media and the modern executive (Downing Street). The modern media (a combination of newspaper and TV moguls and unknown BBC bureaucrats) has usurped the Commons in its erstwhile role of setting the agenda and the tone of British politics, and it, not the Commons, is now the 'forum of the nation'. Our media, not our elected politicians, tell us what is news and what isn't and tell us what is important and what isn't; they are the unrivalled gatekeepers of public debate. This environment, the sidelining of the Commons by the all-powerful London-based media, has led of course to the spawning of the modern public relations industry and the professional manipulation of opinion which now passes for political leadership. It is no wonder that the current Prime Minister's one 'real' job was in public relations.

Just as importantly, the Commons has over recent decades been sidelined by the executive- that is, by office of the Prime Minister in Downing Street. Indeed, today's Commons is a weak institution, emasculated and dominated by the executive operating through the whips and party discipline. The powers of the Prime Minister are considerable. The PM appoints and chairs the Cabinet and government. Alarmingly the PM can still exercise the Royal Prerogative Powers; for still on the books is the ability of Downing Street to make treaties and to go to war. Prime Ministers Major and Blair both contemplated their perfectly legal right to enact the Maastricht Treaty and go to war, the Second Iraq War, bypassing the Commons through the Royal Prerogative Powers. The PM is the one politician who can compete with the media in setting an agenda and mood.

All in all, modern Britain is an executive driven country; unlike the USA, in which the power of the Congress ensures that it is largely legislative driven. Such a powerful executive is doubly troublesome, indeed dangerous, in a country without the safeguards of a written constitution.

Making up the holy trinity of Establishment Westminster is the established church, the Church of England. In a remarkable bravura display the bishops of the Church of England flaunt the very precepts of a modern secular democracy, the separation of church and state, as they take their seats in our legislature and help determine the laws that we need to obey. No other church has a legislative role and there is no role for secularists. Of course, this modern democratic nostrum of separation of church and state is broken, yet again, by the Church of England when it is the Archbishop representing God, and not the Speaker of the House representing the people, who legitimises (by placing the crown on the royal head) our head of state.

Into The Twentieth-Century: How On Earth Did It Survive?

The modern Westminster system was formed by empire and sustained by empire. By the middle of the nineteenth-century Westminster ruled disparate 'nations' or peoples (Irish, Scottish, Welsh) and an increasingly class-ridden England (with the growth of cities and industry to rival country and shires). However, empire was popular amongst the masses. Many of the bottom dogs at home, Celts in the regions and industrial masses in the towns and cities, could take succour in being top dogs abroad with notions of superiority. They could believe that they too, alongside their imperial rulers, possessed colonies and subject peoples with all the attendant superiority complexes. The idea that the peoples of the British Isles were on a par with the black and brown people in the empire (an 'internal empire') ruled over by the same imperial elite in London, never arose (except in Ireland).

As well as the popularity of empire, war, too, served to legitimise the Westminster state. The institutions of the country, no matter how antiquated, were worth fighting for. The idea of British 'greatness', symbolised by the institutions of Westminster, was given a real shot in the arm by 'victory' in two wars. Of course the fact that the Soviet Union and the USA defeated Nazi Germany did not deter 'we won the war' propaganda. In any event, if 'we' didn't actually win the war we were on the winning side; and we did stand alone against Hitler for a year or so.

Pride in the institutions of Westminster, in the monarchy, 'the Mother of Parliaments' and other institutions benefitted from the more general pride in country and the 'British greatness' fantasy. Of course, with the end of empire, and with the fading memory of the world wars, these bonds, never particularly tightly drawn, were bound to loosen.

Still Going: Magic in the 1950s

In many respects the years following the end of the Second World War would seem to have been a great opportunity for constitutional change. The aristocracy, which had lingered into the inter-war period, was well and truly over and the general public was far less deferential, even mildly socialist, in attitude. Just as importantly the reality was of a country about to lose its world-wide empire and become a normal European power. Yet, in 1953 the coronation of Queen Elizabeth - a grand, grandiose and magical ceremony, broadcast to a global audience through the new medium of television - was a clear sign that Britain's postwar establishment (Labour and Conservative) had learnt nothing; they acted as though the country was still a great imperial state ruled by a confident imperial class. All this whilst the reality was that Britain during the cold-war sheltered under the nuclear umbrella of the USA and in security terms at least was a dependency of its former colony.

During the postwar years Britain as a 'great power' (indeed as one of the 'top three') was a myth perpetuated across the Westminster political spectrum as was the superiority of the British constitution ('envied throughout the world'). Indeed during the whole postwar period right up until the turn of the millennium, the idea advanced by reformers that this oldest of old codgers of a constitution needed a thorough overhaul became a decidedly minority concern.

The British leftwing, even during its ascendancy in the 1970s, saw constitutional change as unimportant, a second or third order issue, compared to the country's pressing economic problems. On the right the constitution and its institutions were revered; with many Conservatives suspecting that constitutional reformers, and certainly constitutional radicals, who criticised the monarchy, the House of Lords or 'the Mother of Parliaments' were in some way being unpatriotic.

Postwar Prosperity

Yet, although popular support for the empire and two world wars solidified the legitimacy of Britain's institutions. and thus the Westminster state, in the 1970s an influential section of the British socialist left began to question one of the great Whig tenets - 'parliamentary sovereignty' - arguing that social and economic change could come through mass movements as well as through 'the Mother of Parliaments'. In the 1970s as well, as the UK witnessed a deep, polarising economic crisis (dubbed in the media as a 'crisis of governability') the institutions of the Westminster state began to lose their hold on the public, even to the point where modern institutions born in the postwar years, like the European Union (then the EEC), became more and more acceptable - even seen as a potential future for the people. However, in the late 1980s and during the 1990s, as the country came out of the sense of crisis and decline, and a general feeling of well being, at least amongst 'Middle England' was restored, so too was the standing of the Westminster system and its political class.

Now though, following the 2007-8 global financial crash, and the serious erosion of job security and living standards of many people, the legitimacy of 'the system', including the Westminster state, is once again being questioned. One of the ideas behind the campaign for Scottish independence, both before and after the referendum of 2014, was the notion that staying with Westminster and its seemingly endless austerity programme, would weaken Scottish living standards. It is an idea which could easily gain wider traction amongst the English and Welsh.

Our 'Modern' Ancien Régime: The Myth of Sovereignty.

At the turn of the millennium as Britain looked to the future it did so armed with the most backward constitution in the western world. Britain's New Labour was talking up economic modernisation and social progress but staunchly refusing to look at the fundamental framework governing the country. However, it seemed that, although constitutional change was the product of small groups on the periphery (of Charter 88, Republic and others) it was certainly going to become the wave of the future.

Yet, around this time, there was a new and growing development which ultimately would have a profound effect on Britain's constitutional debate. And this 'something else' was the growth of Euroscepticism from the margins of political life into one of today's major political forces. Modern Euroscepticism is all about 'sovereignty': that is, restoring the 'sovereignty' of the nation by either taking back powers from the EU or pulling out altogether. Restoring 'sovereignty' to Britain has its constitutional aspect (which, of course, is restoring the 'Sovereignty of Parliament') a key nostrum of the failed Westminster state.

No question about it, the Westminster political class likes the nostrum of the 'sovereignty of Parliament' because they do not like sharing power. Never have, never will. Not with the people through a democratic constitution, and certainly not with foreigners, even those in the EU of which we are a full member.

Yet 'Parliamentary sovereignty' in the modern world is an absurd myth. The feudal notion of the English 'sovereign', the King is an outmoded, medieval idea. The related Westphalian notion of 'national-sovereignty' represents a complete misreading of the modern world, of globalisation and its interconnectedness and interdependencies. The fact is that in this day and age a 'sovereign' national Parliaments is simply unable to exercise national decisions whilst the world has integrated markets, whether European or global. In today's world it is arguable that in the lives of Britons the US Fed is more important than the Treasury, and that decisions taken thousands of miles away, let alone in Brussels, have as great an import here as do decisions taken in Westminster. Everything needs to be shared and contingent. In this sense 'national sovereignty' - and the old-fashioned Westminster conception of 'Parliamentary Sovereignty'- are utterly fanciful ideas. They are ostrich-like cries from the past!

Westminster: A Front For 'The New Establishment'

This half-democratic, semi-aristocratic, class-based constitution is perfectly adapted for a British elite transmuting into little more than the management apparatus for a super-rich class and its supporters. As Britain becomes more unequal, a state which is centralised, with power concentrated at the top, and which promotes inequality through its very symbols (monarchy, peers and pomp) sits well with the developing oligarchy.

For a time, during the post Second War years, Westminster was developing into a democratic forum for competing interests and for ideological debate. Working class (Trade unions) and the meritocratic classes (from grammar schools, the London university colleges, the redbrick universities and the polytechnics) were well represented and the traditional upper middle classes (from public schools and Oxbridge) although in key positions, were thought of as a class of the past. These developments are now over. For Westminster today is distancing itself from the people, becoming again a bastion of the old elite, primarily financial and business elites derived from private schooling, who are increasingly shutting out opposition. This narrow route to the top is best exemplified by the fact that in the coalition government elected in 2010 the top four jobs in British politics. Prime Minister Cameron, Chancellor Osborne, Deputy Prime Minister Clegg and London Mayor Johnson were all the products of top public schools and Britain's top two universities. This narrowness of elite recruitment in the UK makes the country stand out amongst other advanced countries. Where else would one school - one school (Eton College!) - provide so many of a country's top political leaders?

As well as being considered 'out of of touch' a more dangerous threat to the legitimacy of the political class is brewing; Westminster is seen as corrupt. The MPs expenses scandal which broke just before the 2010 general election, in itself not particularly egregious was nicely symptomatic of a deeper corruption at the very heart of the Westminster system. This corruption focused on the Commons but actually centres around the Upper House where seats in the Westminster legislature can effectively be bought by judicious donations to party and party front coffers. Other peers sit in the Upper House for no other attribute than a lifetime of keeping on the right side of party leaders; whilst those in the Lower House bend their opinions and votes to the will leaders who could promote them. The hypocrisy is breathtaking. Immersed in the phoney Lords culture of 'honour' and 'nobility' too many of our 'noble lords', who now help make the laws of the land, are actually products of the increasingly grubby world of politics, money and influence.

The New London Establishment: Finance and Media

The political class in Westminster is, though, but the acknowledged aspect of the broader social and financial elite that run the country - an elite increasingly referred to as 'the establishment'. In the 1960s the Tory journalist Henry Fairlie made the term famous and ever since the idea that the country is run by some kind of ruling class, 'an establishment', has been a potent idea. Recently the radical writer Owen Jones has offered this definition: 'Today's establishment is made up - as it always has been - of powerful groups that need to protect themselves in a democracy in which the entire adult population has the right to vote'.[6]

Today's establishment, though, has seen a decided shift in its centre of gravity away from politicians, public sector leaders and of course trade union bosses, towards the private and business sector. As part of this process we have also seen a shift towards London. For the two newcomers to the establishment, indeed key players in the new establishment, are both heavily London based (the finance and media industries).

There can be little doubt that the very beating heart of our new establishment is the London based financial industry in 'the City'. Of course, the finance industry was well represented in the 1960s establishment (as pointed out by essayist Victor Sandelson in Hugh Thomas's 1959 edited book, 'The Establishment').[7] However, since then the City has grown in

---

[6] Owen Jones, The Establishment, and how they get away with it, London, 2014, p.4.

[7] See: Hugh Thomas (ed) The Establishment and Society, London, 1959

relative influence and power within the total economy and society - and has now drawn well ahead of the rest of the country in wealth - and consequently power. A staggering figure tells the story: Inner London's GDP per person is the highest in the whole EU at 328% of the EU27 average - and all this whilst six inner London boroughs are all in the top ten most deprived in the country. London attracts the talent and the high salaries: and migration flows from the rest of Britain into London and the South-East tell the story.

It is hardly surprising therefore that 'the City', its collection of institutions and individuals so dominant in the economy should play a major role in British politics. City figures are not necessarily establishment figures themselves (although some most certainly are). Rather they work both directly and through the wider business community to influence the Westminster political class. Of course they are pushing at an open door. Ever since Labour Leader John Smith in the mid 1990s reversed Labour's stand-offish attitude to business, and in his 'shrimp cocktail circuit' overture courted 'the City', there has been a bi-partisan consensus supportive of the growth of the finance industry and thus the growth of London. Under Tony Blair and New Labour this developed into what amounted in Westminster to a 'fatal attraction' for global finance in London, a virtual alliance with finance carried on by the coalition government following the 2010 general election.

The London Media

Another new boy on the establishment block is the London media industry, its influential elite of moguls, managers and top journalists. Of course, media moguls were at the heart of the 1960s establishment, but at that point there was no developed media elite of top managers and journalists, all on very high salaries who, are now part of a highly self-conscious celebrity opinion forming culture, which helps to set the tone and agenda of national life. From the Guardian and BBC through to the Murdoch Press and the tabloids there is a political consensus behind the neo-liberal values and themes of the finance industry. This was simply not present in the earlier more polarised climate of the 1970s.

This media; elite-concentrated, well-off, London and South-East based, tends to see the world through a prism that is largely southern English to the point where the English provinces; Scotland, Wales and Northern Ireland might well be foreign lands. It was this blinkered view that caused the London media industry to completely miss the post-2010 growing Scottish rebellion against Westminster rule, causing them (rather like the Westminster politicians) to wake up to the issue very late in the day.

A Failing Establishment: And it Nearly Lost the Union to Boot!

This new London-centred finance, media and political establishment, born under Thatcherism and flourished during Blair's New Labour years, has now lost much of its lustre and credibility. The global financial and banking crisis of 2007-8 is widely perceived to be an establishment affair - caused by elite mismanagement or worse. The response - instead of spreading the pain, Britain's rulers have been seen to preside over a sharp rise in inequality both of wealth and income. This sense that 'top people' are the cause of this crisis (it was difficult to blame this crisis, unlike the 1970s crisis, on trade unions and Trotskyites) has set off a wave of anti-establishment rhetoric; and the Westminster politicians have taken the brunt of the criticism and the scorn.

This establishment's failure in the banking crisis was, though, to be compounded by a major political and constitutional failure. For some years, indeed decades, ideas of greater Scottish control over Scottish affairs had been growing. In the

1970s the SNP burst upon the scene as a major party in Scotland. Westminster's response was typical. Power would not be shared, sovereignty would never be conceded. Instead of a federal solution with 'entrenched' powers (as in Germany and the USA) Westminster would remain 'sovereign' and, should the Scots continue to be troublesome, power would be 'devolved'. A proper federal solution to the Scottish problem was rejected as this would mean curtailing Westminster's 'sovereign' power and would cause short-term difficulties, so 'Devolution' became the way out. 'Devolution' suited Westminster as it was rather like a leasehold. It could be 'granted', graciously of course, but also taken back should 'sovereign' Westminster so decide. Indeed Westminster took back powers when Margaret Thatcher's government abolished the Greater London Council by the simple mechanism of an Act of Parliament - an unthinkable action in mature federal states like the USA or Germany (where abolishing Texas or Bavaria, though attractive to some, would in reality never be countenanced).

In 'sovereign' Westminster as support for the SNP and Scottish nationalism grew during the 1990s, 'devolution' to a Scottish Parliament became the answer. Tony Blair's first act in government in 1997 was to introduce 'devolved powers' in the form of the Scottish Parliament, the Welsh Assembly and the Mayoralty of London. Although symbolically important, the powers granted were relatively anaemic. Westminster (in this case both the Treasury and the Bank of England) kept firm control, where it counted - that is control of the economy. Precious Westminster 'sovereignty' was not compromised.

However, after the crash of 2007-8, while the establishment elite presided over declining living standards, the Scottish Parliament, rather than appeasing separatist tendencies, became a launching pad for Scottish independence. After the SNP became the government of Scotland the idea of a referendum on independence gained real momentum. It was at this point that the Westminster elite totally misjudged the situation north of the border. In agreeing to a referendum, the British Prime Minister David Cameron insisted on a straight 'Yes/No', 'In or Out', vote complacently confident that the No vote would easily carry the day, and thus triumphantly reaffirm the union, and Westminster rule. Arguments that 'Devo Max'- shorthand for seriously devolved powers, even Home Rule- should also be in the ballot paper were brushed aside.

Of course, in September 2014, as polling day drew near and it seemed that the Yes campaign might actually carry the day, the Westminster elite, in a display of panic in high places rarely seen before, reacted swiftly. The three party leaders hurriedly agreed to a seemingly united position and jointly 'vowed' to the Scottish electorate that in the event of a 'No' vote not only would the Scottish Parliament be made 'permanent' (a federal concept going far beyond Home Rule) but that it would receive extra powers in a range of policy areas (including taxation). So under pressure were the three party leaders that they enlisted former Prime Minister Gordon Brown to make the case for a 'No' vote in the light of this new 'vow'. Brown, in a major intervention in the campaign, then pledged a strict timetable for the draft legislation that would be enacted during the following Parliament.

In sum, what happened in those mid-September days in 2014 was that the three party leaders, conspiring together over a period of hours, effectively tore up our existing constitution and rewrote it on 'the back of an envelope'. Their dramatic 'new' constitutional proposals were nonetheless deeply confusing and contradictory. On the one hand, by offering to make 'permanent' the Scottish Parliament (a federal concept in which power cannot be taken back) they abandoned the whole devolution process; yet the rest of us remain in a non-federal state. They also handed over extra powers to the Scots on a range of issues, including taxation, which amounted to Home

Rule. All this without any consultation with anyone at all; not party, not parliament, not people.

As this commitment became public many English MPs complained, arguing that England should be granted the same powers as Scotland. David Cameron, just hours after the result was announced, fell into full appeasing mode, and was forced by elements in his own party into another 'back of the envelope' constitutional proposal: 'English votes for English laws'. A constitutional wheeze that he asked former Foreign Secretary William Hague to flesh out and incorporate in a new Bill. Cameron had handed what amounted to the rewriting of the British constitution not to the Parliament or a constitutional convention but to William Hague and a small cabinet committee.

Such was constitution-writing and constitution-making in twenty-first century Westminster. William Hague, for all his abilities, is no Thomas Jefferson; there was to be no deliberation by a wide section of opinion, and no ratification process; in true Westminster style, a club within the Westminster club would decide. Yet again, and drawing upon centuries-long traditions, the political class would change the constitution, such as it was, themselves. In sum, our constitution would remain unwritten and unratified, a plaything for politicians and their immediate political needs. It was banana republic (monarchy) stuff.

So, The Scottish Issue Is Our Chance To Revive the Polity

The situation Westminster found itself in following the Scottish referendum in 2014 was truly desperate. Scotland had voted 'No' in the referendum but only by 10%, meaning that a 5% swing would have secured a 'Yes' victory. Yet, the Westminster politicians had promised 'No' voters a major new settlement. It was clear that should Westminster renege on the promise, and break the vow, then the SNP would revive the whole independence question; either by calling for a new referendum or by contesting the upcoming Westminster elections on a platform that, with an SNP majority of seats from Scotland, would be a green light for a dramatic unilateral declaration of independence. The choice facing the Westminster politicians is now increasingly clear: Either Scotland gets Home Rule or, over time, it secures independence. Either way, England will need a settlement too.

The English Question

The 'English Question' had been the elephant in the room during the Scottish referendum debate, and on the very morning of the result the Conservative Prime Minister responded by pledging to stop Scottish MPs voting on English laws ('English MPs for English Laws'). Of course to allow only English MPs to vote on English laws is a very seductive political argument. Unfortunately, as Professor Vernon Bogdagnor has pointed out, outside of a proper federal constitution, it was well-nigh impossible to operate. First, on the questions of money you cannot divide things neatly between 'matters affecting England' and 'matters affecting Scotland'. With one UK budget whatever English MPs decide on money questions it will automatically have an effect on Scotland. The 'vow' pledged to keep the Barnett formula (which set in stone the financial arrangements between Westminster and Scotland), and thus made any English law which breached the formula redundant.

With Scotland now on the brink - in the union, but threatening to leave if full Home Rule is not delivered - it has become clear that the whole 'Devolution' process engineered by Westminster since the 1970s was fatally flawed. In fact the whole programme implemented in the late 1990s now looks like a typical Westminster ad hoc fudge: another way of putting off problems rather than confronting them by real change. The key design flaw was that 'Devolution' was essentially asymmetrical 'granted' to some parts of the polity (Scotland, Wales, Northern Ireland and London) but not to its largest component, England. This is bound, over time, to stoke up resentment in England, particularly if the devolved power develop into substantial Home Rule in Scotland.

At any rate, by late 2014 the case for an English Parliament (and an English First Minister) was being made vociferously by Conservative and UKIP politicians.

Under the Westminster system such an English Parliament could only come about via the 'Devolution' route, in which the Westminster Parliament would pass an Act 'granting' powers to England as they have 'granted' powers to the Celtic nations. These powers, of course, would not be 'entrenched' and could be taken back by Westminster as happened when London's government, the Greater London Council, was abolished by Mrs. Thatcher in the 1980s. Presumably in any 'Devolution to England' Act Westminster would retain control of functions such as foreign policy, defence and macro-economic policy.

Such an Act would, of course, set up another layer of government as the Westminster Parliament would continue to operate alongside, or above, the new English Parliament. It would entail a separate election (maybe on the same day, maybe not) for each national Parliament and for the Westminster Parliament. The West Lothian question would be resolved - that is, only English MPs would vote on English issues.

However, two fundamental problems stand in the way of achieving an English Parliament this way. First, its powers would not be entrenched, and could be taken back. Without entrenched powers the constitutional landscape would be unclear and the subject of conflict. We might envisage for

Britain a kind of 'Gorbachev and Yeltsin' scenario: in which the Prime Minister in the British Parliament (Gorbachev in The Supreme Soviet), having agreed to an English First Minister (Yeltsin in the Russian Federation) then sees the First Minister take power from him/her as a prelude to a new nation-state called England that would soon take its place in the United Nations and so forth.

Solving The English Question: A Constitutional Convention.

Alternatively, the English Question could be solved not by the usual 'ad hockery' of the opportunistic Westminster political class, but rather by a measured, tried and tested proper constitutional reform process - that is by a constitutional convention leading to a new constitution. This 'proper' process would involve the drawing up of a written constitution which would then be ratified, or rejected, in a referendum of the whole people.

Yet, whenever constitutional theorists mention a written constitution the Westminster political class backs away from the idea- primarily because such a constitution might well lead to the loss of their own power and authority. There are, of course, genuine concerns about drawing up and ratifying a written constitution. It can take time; it will be difficult to get agreement in a polarised political situation. Yet, it is amazing what a sense of crisis will do as we saw in mid-September 2014. When the union looked on the brink of collapse the fractious, warring Westminster politicians managed to set aside differences and come to a constitutional agreement in double quick time.

In my own view we will only come out of this crisis initiated by the Scottish question when we ratify a whole new constitution. 'Ad hockery' and 'back of the envelope' constitutional change will simply not do anymore. What is more, a new constitution would be a splendid opportunity not just to restructure and modernise our system of government; it could bring a sense of renewal and hope to the country.

Writing the constitution could, of course, be assigned to an elected Parliament. However giving the Westminster political class the power to write a new constitution would not be popular and would cause legitimacy problems from the outset. Much better if it is written by a constitutional convention.

Such a convention might well include representatives from all three national 'parliaments', from the great city regions and local authorities of England. The resulting constitution, which would become the basic law of the land and the source of all legitimacy would then need to be ratified or rejected. Of course, it could be decided by the existing Westminster Parliament, but again because of Westminster's low public standing it would be best to have it agreed in a referendum.

The Politics of 'the English Question'

Of course, behind all the arguments about an English Parliament, and more widely 'The English Question', lies the politics of it all. Many English Eurosceptic Tories see such an English Parliament, shorn of MPs from Scotland and Wales, as likely to secure a Conservative majority - and thus continue, in England at least, their 'neo-liberal revolution' and lead ultimately to an exit from the EU ('Brexit'). So, to some extent, the resolution of 'the English Question' and the resolution of 'The European Question' are linked. This helps explain why some Conservative Eurosceptics, like MP Bernard Jenkin, are now so keen on an English Parliament that in order to get one they are even prepared to accept a federal system - a concept most Tories have dismissed and disdained for decades.

Creating a federal system for the British Islands - in which an English Parliament stands alongside Celtic Parliaments - will not necessarily help the 'Brexit' cause. For in any federal system policy functions are divided, Britain's membership of the EU, along with foreign affairs, defence and macro-economic policy would certainly be a federal issue to be decided by the British Federal Parliament, not by the English Parliament. Of course, the views of an English First Minister and Parliament could well be influential but the outcome would depend on the voting strengths of the nations and regions in the British Federal Parliament.

What About 'The North' and the 'Away Counties'.

In an English Parliament the voting power of the 'Home Counties' and rural England would be strengthened as the city-regions of the Midlands and the North could no longer rely upon Scotland and Wales to be a balancing factor. Nor would the 'Away Counties' (now outside London's reach) be able to resist a growing domination by the City of London. To put it in a popular, and populist, imagery: the fear is that the North would end being ruled in perpetuity by the stockbrokers of Surrey. Put in party political terms, the likelihood is that in elections to an English Parliament the Conservatives (and/or UKIP) would do much better than they do in Britain as a whole.

Of course, a Conservative party majority in England is not a foregone conclusion - for in most general elections the Labour Party tends to do well in England when they win in Britain as a whole. Even so, in England alone the Conservatives (or indeed any right-wing government) would be the favourite to win. And in the country's fraught state at the moment it is worth considering that it could well take only one Conservative or Right Wing dominated English Parliament and one

Conservative or Right Wing First Minister to withdraw England from the UK union and then from the EU.

Does England Exist?

Much will depend on how the 'Away Counties' respond to the growing demand for an English Parliament. In other words, will 'the North' agree to continued London rule (assuming that London becomes the seat of an English Parliament)? Will Liverpool and Manchester, Leeds and Sheffield, Birmingham and Coventry, let alone the low income areas of Greater London, accept being forever in a Tory England?

As in the Scottish referendum debate acceptance will depend on perceptions of the economy, upon how majorities in the 'Away Counties' see the economic consequences of staying with the southerners and the City of London.

In the debate about an English Parliament a lot will rest upon the degree of a common English identity. For many 'Englishness' remains one of the world's strongest and most enduring stereotypes and self-images: as one literary critic could write in 1990 'of all the nations we have perhaps the most strongly defined sense of national identity.'[8] Yet, how real is it to think of England like this, as 'one country' (worthy of one legislature and one First Minister)? Or is 'England' simply that part of the UK that is not Scotland, Wales and Northern Ireland? In other words is there such a thing as 'Englishness'? Does, in fact, England exist? My own view is that a common English identity is hugely overdrawn, mainly by elites in the rural south of England and is certainly far less potent than Scottish or Welsh identities.

---

[8] Ian Ousby, The Englishman's England, Cambridge, 1990.

True Brits, Real Identities

Rather than a common identity, one of the remarkable characteristics of England is the continuing strength of its regional and local identities. These identities, many of them in big city-regions- Scowsers, Brummies, Cockneys, Geordies- are still very real; and in some respects are sustained by the phenomenal identification with football teams. Strong, separated identities also exist in the more rural English counties of Cornwall, Devon, Cumbria and in East Anglia. Also, the Southern English 'Home Counties' themselves have something of a common identity - and one that differentiates them from others.

Of course England remains class-ridden, perhaps more so following the global financial crash and the austerity programme. So as 'one nation' still remains something of an aspiration, class distinctions, primarily based upon wealth and income, provide another series of separated identities. As of course do the recent immigrant communities throughout England - even though many recent immigrants now speak with pronounced regional accents. Thus, when looked at this way 'Englishness' becomes a 'tricky' topic. It obviously still means something to many people; but this, as with many national identities, is often a weakening identity drawn from the past. In England's case from that of a particular class at a particular time. In England's case, where common identity was always fairly weak, even non-existent, there has been what might be called a manufactured common identity, imposed on the rest of us and propagated around the world through powerful media myths like that of 'The English Gentleman'.

Indeed, what common identity still exists between Bradford and Buckinghamshire or Liverpool and Littlehampton has certainly been even further weakened over the last few decades as immigration has turned the country from a largely uni-racial society into a multiracial one. Best therefore to look at the whole UK as a great patchwork of cultures and ethnicity, rather than a single common culture. I explored this idea in my essay 'True Brits'.

With regional identity still fairly strong, and in certain parts of the country arguably stronger than 'Englishness', it may seem surprising that the regions and cities of England have tended to resist moves to establish regional governments - most famously in the North East in 2004 when the idea was roundly defeated in a referendum. However, this seeming resistance may have very little to do with lack of a local or regional identity and, still less, an attachment to the centralised Westminster state, and much more because of popular opposition to a further level of government and taxation.

The London Question

Of course, the largest and most prosperous of all Britain's 'regions' is Greater London. In any new federal, or even devolved, system Greater London would be a city-region. But London is a truly global city as well; how would such a global city - linked around the world more intensely than it is linked into the rest of Britain - fit into a new British constitution?

The question again is one of power. Following the Scottish vote the talk is of dispersing power from London to the nations and regions; indeed even supporters of the existing unitary, centralised, state advocate setting up a 'northern powerhouse'. In this process London can hardly be exempted. As London- its Mayor and Assembly - gains more powers how does this affect the rest of the country? Will London become more dominant or less? And will more power for London set in train a push for London to break free from the rest of the country? and even the EU?

The future of London cannot be separated from the broader strategy for the future of the country as a whole. London's role has to centre around national decision-making about the size and role of the country's financial industry. There are two broad visions: one view sees the financial industry in the City as the future of the country. Following the de-industrialisation of the Thatcher-Blair period, and notwithstanding all the problems of the banks, it remains the one success story of the UK. If Britain stays in the EU then the City - providing financial services to the huge EU internal market - and the country can see a path forward for the British economy. On this reading the whole country, including the Scots, should welcome financialisation and not seek to weaken the hold of finance by loosening London's relationship with the rest.

The alternative vision sees a need to re-balance the economy away from financialisation and to re-industrialise initially primarily through New Deal-style big deficit financing or guided QE. This would go hand in hand with an attempt to revivify the industrial power houses of the North and Midland. Such a policy might see London's financial industry taxed more heavily than it is at present as a policy of redistribution is introduced.

In a way the future of London will depend on the extent to which macro-economic policy remains a federal or national function (or how much macro-economic policy remains in the centre). And much will depend upon whether such macro-economic policy remains essentially neo-liberal (London will continue to aggregate power and wealth) or redistributive (in which, after a time, London becomes proportionately less important). Also, in any new regional or national settlement should 'the Home Counties' be added to Greater London to form a large, perhaps too large, a 'London and the South-East' (LSE) region, or should they stand on their own? The politics of this are fascinating. Greater London on its own, and in an even political year, would normally have a smallish Labour majority but the LSE region would be Conservative.

'Capacity Building'

Of course, no-one should be under any illusions about the difficulties of pushing power away from London. The rest of Britain outside London is the victim of decades in which Westminster centralisation has depleted proper local administration throughout the country. In fact, 'devolution' to the regions (or, as in my case here, entrenched regional government in a new federal system) will only succeed with a concomitant commitment to what the modern management idiom calls 'capacity building' in the new regions. If more government is going to be done in these regions then the expertise and organisational acumen that used to be available in the big provincial cities of the country needs to be built up again. This will be no easy task. If the whole of Britain is not to be 'Londonised' then it needs to be started.

A Clean Break: A Federal Future?

As we get to grips with the continuing 'Scottish Question', and then the 'English Question', the ensuing constitutional debate will finally provide us with the opportunity to create a new written constitution not just for Scotland but for the whole country - and thus join the modern democratic community of nations. Creating a new constitution is not just about good governance; it is also about a new start for the country - a clean break with the sense of drift, decline and crisis.

Of course, over the next few years we can continue to stick with what we have; and we can keep patching up a broken system through the tried and failed Westminster system of tinkering in order to survive. If we continue with the present structures of governance of the UK then the crisis of legitimacy facing the Westminster elite and the Westminster system is, by all reasonable accounts, likely to grow - perhaps even to the point where real political extremism could begin to surface.

Of course, critics who support real change can reasonably ask: but how exactly do we get from A to B, how do we actually get from our present de-legitimised system to a new constitution? Who starts the ball rolling? It is not very exciting, but I would suggest that the only realistic way forward is through our existing party system - that is by a political party placing in its manifesto a pledge, should it win the election, to establish a constitutional convention; and then, upon winning, taking on the truly historic task of enacting the legislation that would create the convention (including its composition). This same Act, should it pass, would make provision for the handover of constitutional power. It could, for instance, state that upon the convention successfully completing its work a date would be set by the Parliament and Crown to dissolve itself and vest the ultimate constitutional and legal authority of the country in the new written constitution and the newly constituted bodies of the new constitution.

Alternatively this legislation could stipulate that the new proposed constitution should be subject to a referendum of the British people before it is brought into being.

This new constitution will be written so that all citizens can read and understand it. Our fundamental rules of government will then no longer be so obscure that they need to divined by 'constitutional experts'. As in all other modern democracies a Supreme Court will interpret the rules.

The convention should be free to go in whatever direction it sees fit (subject to some basic democratic principles) such as the democratic accountability of the institutions, the need for citizens rights, the separation of church and state and so on. A provision should be made for amending the constitution. Of course existing laws should continue in force until changed under the new rules.

But within this fundamental framework there should be no sacred cows. Every institution: Parliament, government, the office of Prime Minister, the monarchy, the Supreme Court and so on will be subject to review and the new institutions created should all be subservient to the constitution as the new fundamental law of the land.

This constitutional convention like those great democratic debating sessions in Philadelphia over 200 years ago might well be contentious, and even at times fraught. But at the end of the day, particularly if put to a referendum of the whole people and passed, it will have restored precious legitimacy to our government, and will, at last, allow us to start again.

The Road To A Written Federal Constitution

Drawing up a new written constitution for the British people will, of course, be no small, nor easy, exercise. Should the task fall to a Constitutional Convention then this Convention could of course simply be another name for the Parliament. In less crisis-ridden times this might be acceptable, but not in an era when politicians have lost so much credibility and legitimacy. So, a contemporary Constitutional Convention will need to be drawn from a wide cross section of the public: realistically - speaking this would mean leaders from the nations and regions, from business and trade unions, from the private and public sector, from universities, schools and hospitals, from NGOs and so on, as well as the Westminster politicians.

Of course, such a Convention will likely, just like the Philadelphia convention in the USA over two centuries ago, be a contentious, maybe even raucous, affair - with many competing interests and ideologies fighting it out. In any such convention populist and creative ideas will abound, but, hopefully, they will be tempered by expertise and experience. In drawing up this new constitution those who chair the proceedings will, thankfully, be able to draw not just on our own constitutional development and theories, but also on a wealth of experience from successful existing federal systems. One of the very first decisions to be taken will be whether we should opt for a Parliamentary system (with a Prime Minister) or a Presidential system. Should we go for the former then the German constitution, which British lawyers helped to draw up after the war, would be a good guide.[9] If we opt for a

---

[9] The German constitution, or Basic Law, can be found at https://www.btg-bestellservice.de/pdf/80201000.pdf

Presidential system then the American federal constitution or the constitution of the Fifth French Republic could serve as more than useful guides.[10] My own view is that it would be best to go for a Prime Ministerial System. We are used to it, and the office of Prime Minister could form a familiar core to build around in an otherwise changed constitutional scene.

Another very early decision will centre around whether or not to have a 'federal' constitution; that is to adopt the federal principle that decision-making should be taken at the most appropriate level (with 'big' macro decisions for the central authorities and 'all other' decisions taken at national and regional and local levels). I am assuming here, perhaps fancifully, that this Convention would be taking place after the European Question has been settled in a referendum, and that we are now able to now incorporate European governance into our constitution via the European Treaties we have signed in a formal way by outlining the powers of the EU, such as trade and environment and the like.

A new federal design for Britain would be controversial, not least because of the public perception that such a change would involve a new level of government and new expense (and expenses). As this new exercise would be taking place in the shadow of the global financial crisis and the present era of austerity, public opinion would need to be satisfied that the whole enterprise will serve to cut the cost of the apparatus of government and the size of the political class. This would be a crucial condition but it can easily be met for the Westminster system is seriously over-bloated.

The new design could abolish the over-blown Westminster structure replacing it with a slimmed-down legislature. For

---

[10] The Constitution of the United States can be found at http://www.archives.gov/exhibits/charters/constitution_transcript.html

instance, the curtain could come down on the present House of Lords show (thereby removing over 800 peers, the 26 funnily-named 'Lords Spiritual' could return to solely church duties, and the rest the, 'Lords Temporal' could be re-located say to an empty theatre in London and could work pro-bono). The membership of the Lower House could be reduced from 650 to, say, 400 MPs (the American have only 435 representatives for 300 million people!). The cost of the monarchy and its trappings (including the obscure, and obscurantist, Privy Council) could be substantially reduced- that is, if it the Convention would wish to retain it (and there would be a question here as the conventioneers envisage the reality of Charles Windsor becoming King).

In this suggested new design the Federal level of government would consist of a Lower House (perhaps still called the Commons) of 400 MPs and an Upper House (perhaps called the Senate) of say 100 Senators drawn from the nations and regions. The Prime Minister and Government would be responsible to the Lower House. The Upper House would be a revising chamber, with similar powers to those of the present Upper House, and could be given the function of concurring on treaty-making and supervisory powers over EU legislation. Crucially, the Prime Minister would be responsible to the Lower House of the Federal Parliament and there would need to be provisions for resignation and so on, and for the calling of elections (that is fixed term Parliaments or not). The Prime Minister's powers should be set out clearly.

Of course, such a new design would be a perfect opportunity to relocate the capital outside of London. Suggestions vary from York developing a new Federal Capital Territory around Solway Firth near the M6, building a new M6 Junction, Airport and Parliament & Government buildings. However, it would probably be best, because most cost-effective, to continue to locate the two reduced Houses in the existing Palace of Westminster and the federal government offices in what would be a hugely reduced Whitehall. No grand new offices need be built. Indeed, the Palace of Westminster could be shared by the federal authorities with one of the new regional authorities.

Below the federal government in London would be one layer of government only - the national parliaments of Wales, Northern Ireland and Scotland and in England a number of Regions, City Regions and Rural Regions. These Nations and Regions (which would replace the existing councils) would have their own Parliaments (replacing today's councils), their own First Ministers and cabinets (replacing Leaders and Mayors). These new governments would be entrenched in the new written constitution (that is, like Texas or Hamburg) they would be permanent features, not subject (as in a devolved system, to being abolished). And, to give meaning to their permanence they could be called 'States'.

The 'States' would send - by election or nomination - Senators to the Federal Senate. As for elections, national (that is federal) and State elections could all be held on the same day in some kind of Super-Thursday system; or, alternatively, the Federal elections could be on one day every say five years and the State elections could be staggered as in the US Senate, with a third elected every, say, three years.

The exact number and size of these States (the Regional or City-Regional governments) would be one of the most difficult of the tasks facing any convention. There are, broadly speaking two options: first, to create a number of States based loosely upon the older regional government schemes of the past (all of which have died the death as London-centred centralisation powered ahead); or secondly, to establish a number of big City States (with those local government units outside these City-States being amalgamated into bigger units). All in all, the new design could ensure that no new level of government would be established as the new States would simply be amalgams of existing local government units.

A number of designs for the second tier of government have been put forward over the years by academics, commissions and journalists. Many designs use the former Regional Development Agencies as the basis for future 'States' of England: they were as follows (with population in millions in brackets): South-East (8.6); London (8.1); North-West (7.0); Eastern England (5.8); West Midlands (5.6); South-West (5.2); East Midlands (4.5); North-East (2.5). One analyst, Ian Hackett, has suggested a radical, and no doubt controversial, scheme that, 'with due regard to history, geography and identity', could comprise as well as the 3 national parliaments, 7 parliaments in the new States (Regions and City-Regions) of England. The 11 parliaments would be (with populations): Northern Ireland (1.84m), Scotland (5.3m), Wales (3.1m), Lakeland (7m; Cumbria, Lancashire, Merseyside, Greater Manchester, Cheshire; New Capital: Manchester), Northumberland (7m; Northumberland, Tyne & Wear, Durham, Cleveland, Yorkshire; New Capital: Durham or York), Middle England (15m; all counties not listed in 4, 5, 7, 8 & 9; New Capital: Birmingham), Cornwall (0.54m), Wessex (8m; Devon, Somerset, Dorset, Wiltshire, Hampshire, Berkshire, Surrey, West Sussex; New Capital: Winchester), Essex (12.4m; Greater London, Essex, Kent, East Sussex; New Cap: Westminster) , the Isle of Man (0.09m) and the Channel Islands (0.16m).[11]

But what of the division of powers between the federal and state level? The distribution of powers are crucially important: for they will determine how centralised or de-centralised the British government will be. My own preference is for a de-

---

[11] [11] A concise report on the recent history of English regions can be found at https://en.wikipedia.org/wiki/Regions_of_England. Ian Hackett is a member of the Federal Union.

centralised government that nonetheless allows for the federal or central government to exercise sufficient macro-economic control (to allow, should an elected government so decide, for a good degree of redistribution between London and the rest of the country). In the new written constitution the powers (functions) of the Federal government as a whole (the two Houses and the executive branch led by the Prime Minister) should be clearly set out, and could include:

- Foreign and Security policy
- Macro-Economic policy
- Treaty-Making

The powers of the States (that is the three national Parliaments and the other Parliaments) could be simply stated, as in the US constitution, as 'all those powers not allocated to the Federal government. Alternatively, should the Convention want a different bias to the system then the powers of the 'the States' could be set out and 'all other powers' could be allocated to the Federal Parliament. It would also be properly transparent and democratic to outline the powers that have been vested in the EU by various treaties, and also state, as many modern constitutions do, that treaties take precedence over domestic law.

The convention would need to take a view on another important, arguably the most important, institution in the country in an era when monetary policy is dominant - the Bank of England. One of the delights of constitution-making is that it will present the British body politic with the ability to decide whether bankers should control the economy. The central bank could be brought back under political control either by returning it to the Treasury or keeping it independent but subjecting it to serious democratic control, say through its governors and leading members being selected by a committee of the Lower House, and, according to performance, being subject to recall. Of course, if neo-liberal ideas are still in the ascendant in the Convention then it will, no doubt, be left as it is. Under any provenance it should have its role and limits clearly set out.

The convention would also need to decide on the question of 'rights'. Constitution-making is a perfect opportunity to entrench rights and to make them inviolable. But the scope of rights will be contentious. Should we stipulate political and judicial rights only or social and economic ones too? As will be the mode used to interpret them. Should we leave 'rights' to law or should we elevate them to constitutional rights? What of incorporating the European Convention into the constitution, thereby entrenching it?

Of course, the constitution would need to clearly state where authority lies in the crucial role of interpreting the written constitution. This would normally fall to a Supreme Court and such a Court could, to maintain some democratic legitimacy, be nominated by the office of the Prime Minister but, say, ratified by the Upper House. A crucial point here would be the role in the constitution of the European Court of Justice (the ECJ) and the European Court of Human Rights (ECtHR). If the country's relationship with the EU has been settled by the time the Convention meets then, if we remain in, this would be a good time to set out clearly the exact legal and constitutional power of the ECJ within Britain's constitutional arrangements.

[Editors note: The European Court of Human Rights is an institution of the Council of Europe (CoE) and is separate from the European Union. It's worth bearing in mind that the UK may leave the EU but remain in the CoE, there are 19 countries which are signatories to the European Convention of Human Rights (such as Russia, Turkey and Switzerland) but not in the European Union.]

Also, as constitutions are living documents and should be open to change, there would need to be some constitutional provision not just for the powers of a Supreme Court but for the important task of amending the constitution - say by two thirds of the Lower House and one half plus one of the Upper House or by a simple majority in both Houses and two thirds of the States.

In conclusion, I need to deal with the criticism - levelled by old fashioned theorists in Westminster - that written constitutions are somehow inflexible and unable to move quickly to accommodate change. No matter its provenance - from those who share a unwritten constitution system with Saudi Arabia - at face value, of course, there is something in this. But not much; as countries who have adapted to change much more successfully than we have all have written constitutions. What proper constitutions do is take ultimate authority away from the political class by laying down basic rules of the game. Within this framework proper national constitutions certainly allow for the winds of social and economic change. For instance, one such wind blows in today from abroad in the form of globalisation, market integration and, in Europe, the EU; but in Britain's case our unwritten rule of 'parliamentary sovereignty' has no way of dealing with this new integrationist reality. Ultimately Written constitutions can incorporate global changes, indeed if need be make them ascendant through treaty-making rules or the changing interpretation of the rules by the Supreme Court (which does not have to be dominated by lawyers and legalistic thinking). Secondly, constitutions can reflect, not hinder, political change, even radical political change. All they ask, and reasonably so, is that it takes place 'constitutionally, and with due regard to democratic processes. One of the great, often unspoken fears about Westminster's unwritten constitution and 'old boys' culture is that, as it is not bound by entrenched democratic rules and is at the whim of a temporary political class without constraint, it has no defences against an extremist authoritarian cabal to taking over.

In any event, in Britain's present circumstances, the great benefit of a proper constitution is that it will allow us to finally take power out of the hands of our self-sustaining establishment and political class and place it in the hands of 'the people' - meaning in real terms of course in the hands of a wide cross-section of the British public. Creating such a constitution, no matter how difficult, would re-invigorate our tired and cynical democracy. It is a chance for renewal.

WAR MAKING AND THE RIGHTS OF PARLIAMENT

Introducing a written constitution to grant Parliament the right of a vote before the country goes to war.

By Graham Allen MP.
Edited and formatted by Junade Ali.
Published by the Reform Foundation.

Editor's Note

In Britain, even to this day, there is no requirement for the Prime Minister to consult Parliament before declaring war on a foreign country. In fact when a Prime Minister is gracious enough to give Parliament a say the matter of war and peace it is nothing but a courtesy.

Royal Prerogative powers allow the government to exercise the monarch's numerous powers to carry out policy including issuing and revoking passports, appointing government ministers, making treaties, recognising states and, as discussed in this paper, going to war.

Graham Allen is one of the few Members of Parliament to represent the constituency in which he was born as the Labour MP for Nottingham North. In addition to this he has held a number of parliamentary and front-bench positions, including as whip to the Deputy Prime Minister and later the Chancellor of the Exchequer. He still regards himself as 'a recovering whip, taking one day at a time'.

Having been elected in 2010 as Chair of the House of Commons Select Committee on Political and Constitutional Reform, his ambition is to turn the UK into a democracy. He has written 'Reinventing Democracy' and 'The last Prime Minister; being honest about the UK Presidency'.

Damned as 'very independent minded' by No.10, he proved it in opposing the war in Iraq by helping to organise the two biggest parliamentary rebellions within a governing party in political history.

One of the few positive outcomes of the UK joining the invasion and occupation of Iraq from 2003 involved the powers of Parliament. During the lead-up to the conflict, and particularly with the votes to approve the action in the Commons of February and March 2003 – which were the occasion for the two largest rebellions in modern parliamentary history – elected representatives began to extract an important concession to democracy from a reluctant executive. It involved a set of powers known as the Royal Prerogative.

These government authorities were once exercised on the individual will of the monarch. Now most of them are in practice deployed by ministers, especially the Prime Minister. They include the ability to conduct diplomacy, to instigate inquiries, to issue and revoke passports, and the right of the Prime Minister to hire and fire ministers, and allocate their portfolios. One of the most prominent Royal Prerogative powers is to commit the armed forces into action overseas, either with or without a full declaration of war being issued (something which does not take place nowadays).

This important range of powers has never been approved by Parliament, and Parliament does not have a formal role in the way they are exercised. This position is clearly unacceptable in a democracy, because of the unaccountable discretion it provides to the executive. It is curious that we are often told how important is Parliamentary sovereignty to our constitution, and how we need to preserve it against all threats – yet the sovereignty I and my colleagues in Westminster supposedly exercise on behalf of the public does not extend to matters such as our relations with foreign states, or the appointment of ministers.

The Iraq invasion of 2003 was important from the point of view of the prerogative war powers. Because of the controversial nature of the action, a body of opinion built up in the Commons that MPs had to have a close role in the policy as it developed. In September 2002, Tony Blair began to indicate publicly that he intended to join George Bush in a venture in Iraq but the House was in recess and could not be recalled without the consent of the government. I was able to gain the support of a cross-party group of colleagues for the idea of calling our own rebel Parliament, the threat of which was enough to force No.10 to back down and agree to an official reconvening of Parliament.

Political pressure also obliged ministers to concede that they would not act without first consulting the Commons explicitly on their intended course of action. It is shocking to think that this idea should have been novel at the time, and that major conflicts in which we have taken part – for instance, both world wars, and more recently the intervention in Afghanistan from 2001 – were embarked upon without prior Commons approval of a substantive motion. While those of us who opposed the Iraq war were not ultimately able to stop it, we had at least established an important precedent – which is often the best that can be obtained under the unwritten UK constitution.

The Iraq precedent is now beginning to turn into a fully blown constitutional convention. Importantly, in August 2013, in another emergency recall, the Commons was asked to approve in principle the possibility of an intervention in Syria. Showing they were more than a rubber-stamp – and to the evident irritation of the executive – MPs had the audacity to vote down the government motion. Though the Prime Minister, David Cameron, had the legal authority to proceed without specific approval from Parliament, politically this option was not viable. The action was halted before it began.

While this development in the power of Parliament is welcome, we should not assume it is secure. A convention is not the same as a legally enforceable right. The executive still has the initiative in deciding when precisely it will seek parliamentary approval, and on what terms. It can also, if it sees fit, choose not to consult Parliament at all before an action commences, perhaps arguing that emergency circumstances prevent it from doing so. The debate and vote on a substantive motion over Libya on 21 March 2011 took place only after the intervention was announced on 18 March. There are numerous grey areas where it is not clear whether parliamentary consent is required: for instance, over sending military advisers not ostensibly intended for a combat role. Such missions can creep. A clear danger is that they could become fully-blown combat operations, without Parliament having approved the initial deployment.

One means of eliminating these troubling uncertainties about the position of Parliament with respect to the war powers would be to place arrangements on a statutory basis, giving MPs a clear legal right to approve and oversee the use of troops in potential or actual combat roles overseas. It could clearly define the exceptions to the rule, allowing for instance for rapid responses to surprise attacks, with only retrospective consent required in such circumstances. Parliament could then have the powers it needs, and the executive the discretion it needs, while the ability of either party to abuse its rights would be reduced. A useful model to follow here is the United States 1973 War Powers Resolution (or Act), that provides rights for Congress in relation to military interventions that do not amount to full declarations of war. We hoped in Parliament that the UK was about to adopt this kind of measure when the Foreign Secretary, William Hague, committed to introducing legislation defining the role of Parliament in the Libya debate of 21 March 2011. However, the government has not yet delivered on this promise and is unlikely to do so any time soon.

Reform of the Royal Prerogative is possible. It has happened in a number of areas over the last few decades. For instance, the intelligence and security agencies, which previously existed under the prerogative, were moved to a statutory basis in the 1980s and 1990s; while the Civil Service was subject to a similar reform in 2010. But we have waited a long while for elected representatives to be given clear rights in the making of decisions that are as important as any country can make: to go to war. It is now time to consider whether a better way exists of addressing the problems raised by the persistence of the Royal Prerogative, in armed conflict as other areas. Nearly every other democracy deals with many of these issues in its written constitution, which seems the most appropriate place for them. But the UK has no such text. Only by introducing a written constitution will it be possible fully to establish the principle that the executive derives all its powers from the people, and that it is accountable to them and their representatives for the way it uses them.

www.ingramcontent.com/pod-product-compliance
Lightning Source LLC
Chambersburg PA
CBHW072246170526
45158CB00003BA/1015